A *Family* Genogram Workbook

Israel Galindo

Elaine Boomer

Don Reagan

A Family Genogram Workbook
Israel Galindo, Elaine Boomer, Don Reagan

ISBN 10: 0-9715765-3-X

ISBN 13: 978-0-9715765-3-7

A FREE **GROUP STUDY GUIDE** FOR THIS WORKBOOK IS AVAILABLE FROM THE EDUCATIONAL CONSULTANTS WEB SITE: www.galindoconsultants.com.

Published by Educational Consultants
www.galindoconsultants.com

Printed in the United States by Morris Publishing
3212 East Highway 30
Kearney, NE 68847
1-800-650-7888

Contents

Introduction

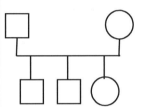

This workbook is an introduction to the genogram, an exciting and fun tool for understanding your family and your place in it. By using this workbook you will learn how to create and interpret your family genogram. Along the way you will also learn some of the basic principles of family systems theory.

A genogram is a diagram of your family. It contains information you would typically find on a multi-generational family tree or genealogy such as names and the dates of birth and death for each individual. In addition, a genogram is organized to illustrate important individual characteristics such as personality, vocation, and health. However, genograms dramatically depart from genealogies in the representation of family relationships. While a family genealogy will give you basic information about a marriage and the offspring of that marriage, a genogram uses specific symbols to depict the *emotional* relationships of those same individuals and the *emotional relationship patterns* of the family system to which they belong. For example, a genogram can show if a marriage was happy or troubled and if a child had a close relationship with the mother but was distant from the father. It can also show how a relationship came to be as a result of multigenerational patterns of family behavior due to family history, values, or as a result of anxiety surrounding crises. This is the real power of a genogram and the way it can provide a pathway to greater understanding of your family and yourself.

Creating your genogram will help you understand the other members of your family better, but the primary goal is an enhanced understanding of yourself. There is no greater shaping influence on our lives than the families that raised us. Families influence and establish patterns of behavior that we are not even aware of. In fact, we rarely realize that these patterns are passed on from generation to generation. Families teach us how to function in society and how to relate to others. From our families we learn how to be a friend, a lover, a spouse, a parent,

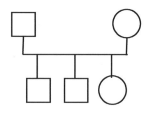

and a worker; how we approach spirituality, faith, and religion; how we go about problem solving and whether we are more likely to project positive or negative attitudes. Our family of origin influences everything from language to mannerisms. This is obvious by the very different ways that particular families interact. One family may have a largely non-verbal, non-confrontational way of interacting. Meanwhile, its neighbors may have a very loud and provocative style. When individuals from these two different families meet, it is likely that their patterns of interactions will make for awkward moments if not misunderstandings or difficulties. While these family influences do not dictate exactly what we will become in a deterministic sense, they do supply us with most of the raw material that we have to work with in life.

Most of the time we act, or react, in an automatic fashion based on these family influences. Studying your genogram will allow you to identify the source of these influences and bring what is normally automatic and unconscious to the forefront. In this way you can begin to identify both the strengths and weakness in the functioning of your family. This awareness gives you the opportunity to choose to rely on the identified strengths rather than to function automatically in patterned negative behaviors, thoughts, or attitudes. Over time, it may even be possible to establish new positive patterns of behavior and new ways of thinking. Choosing different ways of behaving can be extremely difficult because of the power of family influences that shaped us. However, even if it is only done occasionally, the ability to *choose* to act, rather than react, outside our patterned ways of functioning can bring greater emotional health to our families.

Your genogram will highlight the interdependence of your family members. Looking at your family as an interdependent whole, rather than a group of individuals functioning apart and independent from the other family members, is at the heart of family systems theory. (The concepts of family systems theory can also be applied to other systems that often function like families, such as work systems and congregations.) Your genogram work will allow you to see more clearly how the behavior of one family member influences the behavior of the other family members. Sometimes this will be true generation to generation!

How a genogram is constructed and interpreted is a function of the creator of the genogram. There is no single genogram for any one family (as you will see, you can even create different genograms according to "themes"). Each family member can, and probably will, have a different perspective on the relationships in the family. This is entirely fine and should not deter you in creating your own genogram, or from sharing it with your family. Your genogram is for your benefit. It is your tool to achieving a greater understanding about yourself.

How To Use This Workbook

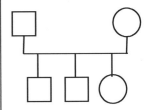

This book is organized to get you started on your genogram right away. Chapter 1 introduces common genogram symbols and the rules for creating your genogram. Use the worksheets in Chapter 1 to create your own genogram. We can think of no better way to begin than to jump right in! As you construct your genogram you will probably begin to see patterns and key events in your family that you were unaware of. Read through Chapter 1 in its entirety before beginning your genogram.

The rest of the chapters will guide you in using your genogram to interpret your family with increasing depth. Chapter 2 provides a basic introduction to understanding different family situations and relationship patterns and the power that past generational patterns can have on your current generation. Additionally, Chapter 2 emphasizes the impact of gender and birth order on family functioning. Chapter 3 contains a series of questions intended to help you apply the concepts introduced in Chapter 2 to your own situation. These questions will inspire you to dig deep when using your genogram. Chapter 4 provides a fuller explanation of family systems theory concepts, building on the basics of chapters 2 and 3. In addition, Chapter 4 offers ideas and strategies to employ in gathering your genogram information, including family "interviewing" techniques. For those desiring a deeper study of the concepts introduced in this workbook we offer a bibliography of good books on the subject and of other books that are written from a family systems point of view.

Chapter 1

How To Diagram Your Family Genogram

Family emotional process refers to the ways that a family system works by how the members of the family relate to each other on an emotional level related to beliefs, patterns, anxiety, multigenerational family history, triangles, and homeostasis.

A genogram is a graphic representation (a diagram) of family members and their relationships over at least three generations. It can look very much like a family tree or a genealogy chart; however, it is more than just genealogical information. Genograms include information about the *kinds* of relationships that exist between family members. In addition, genograms depict critical and nodal events in the family's history and information about the family itself as a whole, particularly as related to the family life cycle and what is called "family emotional process."

A genogram is a tool for understanding how your family works. Creating and studying your family genogram will help you understand what kind of family you come from. It will reveal why your family functions the way it does, and why the individual members of your family, including yourself, have come to be the way they are as a result.

A genogram can illustrate patterns of behavior in families that are otherwise invisible and go unnoticed. In order to discover and depict these family "patterns" (the ways that family members relate to each other, illnesses, recurring behaviors), you'll need to initially create a genogram that depicts at least three generations. The more generations your genogram contains the better, but start with at least three.

Genogram Basics

When you create your genogram you map out a basic diagram of family members in relation to you by using symbols and lines. These symbols and lines are illustrated later in this chapter.

Typically the genogram is drawn on a single piece of paper. A large piece of poster board is often suitable. It is a good idea to create a trial draft or two before attempting a more permanent version. It can take some practice to learn how to space the symbols appropriately. Earlier generations are pictured at the top of the paper and the present generation is at the bottom. Your father's side of the family is usually to the left and your mother's side of the family to the right. Individuals of the same generation are depicted on the same level. Siblings are illustrated oldest to youngest from left to right. The dates for birth, death, marriage and divorce are included. Other symbols are then used to designate individual traits or characteristics (See page 11 for a sample genogram).

After you have completed the basic structure and information about individuals, you will continue by drawing symbols and connecting lines that represent the relationships between family members. You will use these symbols and lines to show excessive closeness (enmeshment), distance, conflict, triangles, and balance.

To create your family genogram, "build" the diagram following this order:

1. **Yourself**. Start by drawing yourself in the center of the page using the appropriate symbol. Use double lines for your symbol to make it clear from whose perspective the genogram is being drawn. All other individuals will be drawn with single lines. Record your name, date and place of birth and your age. You may include your health status, education level, and occupation.

2. **Your Parents**. Draw appropriate symbols for your parents and other partners in this generation. Your father should be on the left and your mother on the right. Record their names, status, ages and dates of birth. You may also record their current place of residence or place of origin, health status, educational level, occupation, and dates and causes of death if deceased (see page 8).

3. **Your Siblings**. Add your siblings from left to right, oldest to youngest, keeping yourself in the correct birth order. Include their names, ages (or dates of birth) and the dates and causes of death if deceased. Diagram their marital status and children, if any. Include the following if they are important family issues: health status, places of residence, vocation, etc. (see page 8).

The following are computer software programs that create genograms. These follow the conventions and symbols of the genogram and can even plot the lines of relationship in a family.

GenoPro
(www.genopro.com)

Wonderware
(www.interpersonal universe.net)

SmartDraw
(www.smartdraw.com)

GenoWare
(www.genogram.org)

BASIC SYMBOLS KEY

Male: □

Female: ○

You: □ or ○

Deceased: ⊠ ⊗

Male: ☐

Female: ○

You: ☐ or ○

Deceased: ⊠ ⊘

Alcoholism or drug abuse:

Mental or emotional illness:

Identified patient:

[1] Cutoff or "emotional cutoff" refers to attempts by one family member to cutoff all emotional contact with another. Geographical distance is not required as, often, cutoff family members may occupy the same house.

4. **Your Spouse.** Add your spouse and previous partners as appropriate. Indicate your current marital status, and record the dates of marriages, separations, and divorces. For each spouse or partner, indicate the name, age or date of birth, and date and cause of death if deceased (see page 9).

5. **Your Children.** Add your children. Record each child's name, age (or date of birth) and date and cause of death if deceased. Include other issues of importance: health status, place of birth or residence, vocation, etc. (see page 8).

6. **Your Grandchildren.** Add your grandchildren, completing the drawing as for children.

7. **Your Grandparents.** Add your grandparents and all pertinent details.

8. **Other Important People.** Add aunts, uncles, cousins, other relatives and any non-relatives who are very important to your family. Place these persons on the genogram and include pertinent information for them.

9. **Individual Symbols.** Next, add symbols for significant issues in your life or the family's life. If there is a history of substance abuse, mental illness, obesity, or disease, for example, you will add symbols to signify which family members were affected. You can be as creative as you want at this point, like using color. Use one color to illustrate a history of illness, and if there is a history of abuse, show that with a different color.

10. **Relationship Lines.** Finally, use the relationship lines to indicate how the individuals in your family related to each other: distance, enmeshment, abuse, closeness, conflict, cutoff[1], etc. Be sure to indicate where the significant emotional triangles were in the family system (see page 10).

Information To Include In Your Genogram

Below is a list of the information you want to include in your genogram. Except for basic information you do not need to include all of these on one genogram. Sometimes you will want to create different genograms with different emphases. Add information as it becomes appropriate and useful.

1. Names, nicknames, family titles for each person. You may also include Meyers-Briggs Personality type or Enneagram number.[1]

2. Dates of birth, death, severe illness, marriages, separations, divorces, other rites of passage.

3. Physical locations, place of birth, and dates of important moves.

4. Type of relationship and contact between members of the extended family or strength and type of relationship.

5. Emotional cutoffs. What was the issue or event? When?

6. Ethnicity, occupation, socioeconomic level, education, religious affiliation and participation.

7. Triangles (see p. 23), power struggles, alcohol and/or drugs problems, mental illnesses, chronic diseases, Identified Patient,[2] suicide, or health problems.

8. Other significant health and personality characteristics like frequent or significant hospitalizations, depression, etc.

The Basic Symbols of the Genogram

Following the general convention ("rules") for depicting your genogram is important. By carefully following the rules of the genogram design you'll be able to create a diagram that is instantly understandable. This will allow for quicker interpretation and an intuitive way to spot patterns. Following the standard rules will also allow you to share your genogram with others more easily.

Before you start creating your genogram, take the time to familiarize yourself with the basic "building blocks" for the genogram. Refer to the symbols key page (p. 12) when working on your genogram. In addition to the basic symbols that depict the individuals in your family you will find symbols that represent the typical ways that people in families relate to each other: close, distant, conflictual, cutoff, etc.

On the following pages you will find a guide to the basic symbols to use in your genogram. Take some time to study the symbols so you'll be familiar enough to know what they represent and how a genogram is put together.

[1]The Enneagram is a personality types model. It depicts the nine basic personality types. Used by therapists, spiritual directors, and novelists, the Enneagram can be a helpful tool for understanding the interplay of personalities in a family. See the bibliography for books on the subject.

[2]An Identified Patient refers to a person in the family who becomes the focus of attention as a way to detract from the real problem in the family. This person may be a "scapegoat," perceived as the troublemaker or a weak and dependent person. An Identified Patient (IP) often exhibits symptoms, from acting out to illnesses.

GENERAL FAMILY CONVENTIONS

Males are depicted with a square symbol and females are depicted with a circle.

The male is generally placed on the left of the marriage dyad. Show the marriage relationship with a solid line connecting the two as depicted.

Depict children in the family by birth order, with the first born/oldest on the left. In this example, the married parents have three children, the oldest of which is a male, the second child (who is also the middle child) also a male, and the youngest being a female.

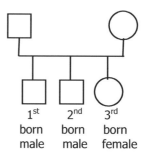

OTHER BIRTH CONVENTIONS

You can depict particular birth associations using the following symbols. The consistent use of these conventions makes it easy to instantly understand the birth situation of a person in the family (remember, all squares represent males, all circles represent females).

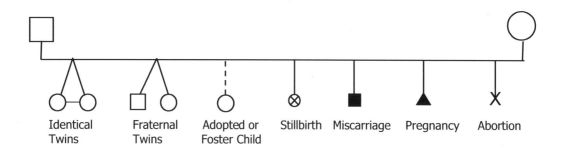

MARITAL CONVENTIONS

Couples that are not married (engaged or living together) are depicted with a dashed line.

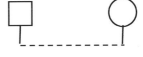

Record the date of marriage on the solid line connecting the spouses as shown.

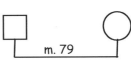

A **separation** of a married couple is depicted with one slash. Include the date of separation if you know it.

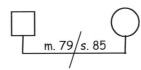

The **divorce** of a couple is shown with two slashes. Record the year of the divorce on the marriage line.

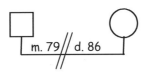

A **death** is depicted by an X in the person's symbol. Record the birth and death years of persons over their symbol. A **remarriage** is depicted by a new marriage line including the date of the marriage.

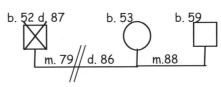

Note how even this simple genogram can provide a lot of information. Just by looking at this small diagram we know that this couple was one year apart in age, they were married in 1979 in their 20s, the marriage lasted seven years ending in divorce in 1986. The couple had no children. The man died one year after the divorce and the woman married two years after the divorce (and one year after the death of her former husband). We can see that she married a much younger man than her former husband.

INDIVIDUAL TRAITS CONVENTIONS

Below are conventional symbols to depict individual traits and characteristics. Depict as many of these traits on your family genogram as you are able given the information you have.

Mental Illness or Physical Illness   Alcoholism or Drug abuse   Deceased with age at time of death   Indicate current age of individuals inside symbol

The power of the genogram is not that it can depict a lot of family information in an efficient manner, but that you can depict the dynamics of what is going on in the family in a way that is easily interpreted. Depicting the relationships among family members is done through the use of relationship symbols. Use the symbols below to show the relationship among family members.

Closeness between two persons is depicted by a double solid line between the persons' symbols. In this example the mother is close to the middle son.

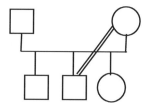

Stronger emotional bonds and relationships are depicted with additional lines. A very **close** relationship is depicted with a double line, while **fusion** (enmeshment) is depicted with a triple line. In this example, the father is very close to the daughter, and fused with the mother, while the mother has a close relationship with the middle child.

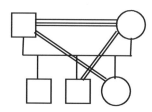

Tense and anxious relationships in the family are depicted in various ways. When there is a **cutoff** between members use an interrupted line between the parties. Here is a married couple that is experiencing a cutoff.

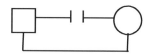

Depict **conflict** between persons with a zigzag line. Emotional distance between persons is shown with a dashed line. Depict emotional **distance** as a dashed line. In this example we see a family in which the mother and daughter are in conflict and the father is distant from the wife and the second-born son.

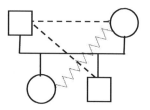

You can combine certain relationship lines to depict complex relationship dynamics. For example, you can depict a relationship that is **fused and conflictual** by combining the conventions for each. In this genogram we see that the relationship between the mother and daughter has shifted and escalated from merely conflictual to fused and conflictual.

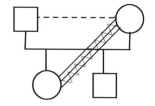

Below is a sample completed genogram with four generations. Your genogram will look similar to this in structure and in the use of the conventional symbols. Study the genogram and see how much information you can interpret about this family in terms of (1) basic information about the family, and (2) what is going on in the relationships within the family. Since **Anne** is the principle person for this genogram she is indicated by an emphasized gender symbol.

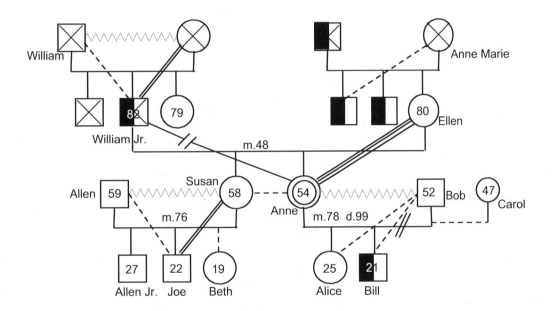

What observations do you make about:

- Relationships?

- Illness and/or addictions?

- Separations and/or cutoffs?

- Birth order and sibling position?

- Intergenerational patterns?

- Names?

- Anne's relationship with her family?

- Can you identify the triangles in this family system (see p. 23)?

- What additional information can this genogram include?

You can refer to the key on this page as you develop your genogram. Be consistent in the use of symbols so that your genogram will be easy to interpret.

BASIC SYMBOLS

Male	☐
Female	◯
Married	
Unmarried couple	
Separation	
Divorce	

RELATIONSHIPS

Close	
Conflictual	
Close bond	
Enmeshed	
Emotional cutoff	
Abuse	
Enmeshed conflictual	

BIRTH IDENTIFICATION SYMBOLS

Pregnancy	▲
Adopted	
Twins	Identical Fraternal
Abortion	
Stillbirth	⊗
Miscarriage	●
Gender unknown	◇

CONDITION SYMBOLS

Present age	23	54
Death		
Alcohol or drug addiction		
Mental or emotional conditions		
Identified Patient		

GETTING STARTED

Now that you understand the basics of drawing a family genogram it's time to create your own! Use the following work pages to create your family genogram. Follow the rules and conventions as best you can, but don't worry too much about getting it perfect. Remember to start with yourself and with your family of origin, move on to your immediate family, then to the previous generations as best you can.

Gather as much information as you can before you begin. Then, solicit additional basic information from your family members. Working on your genogram will eventually move you toward your family to talk about how the family works and how it shaped its individual members. We'll talk more about that in subsequent chapters.

For right now, jump right in and start creating your genogram! Start with a basic genogram, then make as many versions as you like. For example, you may want to create a family health history genogram, or an education and career genogram. Another genogram can focus on family migrations and geographical moves. If religion and faith is a significant family trait you can create a genogram to plot its impact on your family across the generations. Certainly you can plot all of those factors into one major genogram if you are ambitious. However, when starting out, simpler is better.

Once you complete your genogram continue to Chapter 2 to begin interpreting your family relationships.

POSSIBLE THEME GENOGRAMS

- Family health history
- Education & careers
- Migrations & moves
- Religion and faith
- Longevity (age at time of death)
- Cutoffs
- Father-son relationships
- Mother-daughter relationships
- Father-daughter relationships
- Mother-son relationships
- Sibling relationships
- Military service
- Violence and lawlessness
- Male roles
- Female roles
- Enneagram or personality types
- Individual family roles
- Etc.

BASIC SYMBOLS KEY

Male:

Female:

You: or

Deceased:

Alcoholism or drug abuse:

Mental or emotional illness:

Identified patient:

Close

Very close

- - - - - - - - - -

Distant

Enmeshed

Conflicted

Conflicted-enmeshed

Cutoff

BASIC SYMBOLS KEY

Male:

Female:

You: or

Deceased:

Alcoholism or drug abuse:

Mental or emotional illness:

Identified patient:

RELATIONSHIP KEY

——————————
Close

══════════
Very close

– – – – – – – –
Distant

≡≡≡≡≡≡≡≡
Enmeshed

/\/\/\/\/\/\/\/\/\/\
Conflicted

/\/\/\/\/\/\/\/\/\/\
Conflicted-enmeshed

———⊣ ⊢———
Cutoff

BASIC SYMBOLS KEY

Male: ☐

Female: ○

You: ☐ or ◎

Deceased: ☒ ⊘

Alcoholism or drug abuse: ▤ ◓

Mental or emotional illness: ◧ ◑

Identified patient: ☐ ○

RELATIONSHIP KEY

———————————————
Close

═══════════════
Very close

– – – – – – – –
Distant

≡≡≡≡≡≡≡≡≡≡
Enmeshed

∧∧∧∧∧∧∧∧∧∧∧∧∧
Conflicted

∧∧∧∧∧∧∧∧∧∧∧∧∧
Conflicted-enmeshed

————⊣ ⊢————
Cutoff

Chapter 2

How To Interpret Your Family
Using The Genogram

Diagramming your family using a genogram is a good first step to understanding your family, your place in it, and how it helped you become the person you are today. You probably have already gained insight into your family just by creating your family genogram. Now let's explore a few key concepts to help you interpret your family's emotional system. A family's emotional system consists of the family beliefs and values, the ways of relating to one another, and the relationship patterns that develop to deal with anxiety, change, and crises. Family emotional systems also include things like sibling position (birth order), the quality and kind of parental and marital relationships, and the patterns of relationship associated with those factors. Interpreting your family system will help you to identify your individual patterns of functioning, the family influence that impact the choices you make and the emotional "hot buttons" that cause you to be reactive.

Be curious and open-minded as you begin to interpret your family genogram. Remember that there is no right or wrong to any one family member's beliefs, attitudes or perspectives about the family. It is important, therefore, to ask as many family members about their perceptions regarding the family stories and relationships. Expect family members to have different perceptions and recollections about family events and appreciate that, more often than not, no one perspective is more "right" than another. Getting various opinions simply gives you more information to think about the family system as a whole. Sometimes asking family members about their perceptions and memories can be a "touchy" process. Some family members may be reluctant to talk about sensitive issues or to reveal what they consider to be "negative" information. Be considerate and sensitive to this but be persistent. Often the first few times you talk to a family member about your genogram project you will get little or no information, but by asking again or in a different way, you can have success.

Creating a family genogram and interpreting it takes time and effort that can span several months or even years as you talk to more family members and gather more information. Keep in mind that it is not the genogram in and of itself that is important; rather, it's what you learn and understand about your family and how that impacts you. A family genogram is like a puzzle with interlocking pieces representing individuals, data, beliefs, behaviors and repetitive patterns. These puzzle pieces will eventually come together to transcend a focus on individual family members and provide a clearer, more complete picture of your family's emotional system.

Relationship Patterns

Once you have drawn your genogram and identified the primary relationship patterns by using the symbols presented in Chapter 1, you can begin to see the ways that family members relate to one another. These patterned ways of relating become like "scripts" with the family "actors" performing their parts without conscious thought. They are repetitive in nature (and therefore predictable) and inform the functioning of both the individual members of the family and the family as a whole, especially during periods of heightened anxiety. Moreover, family members often function one way with a particular person in the family and in a completely different way with another person following distinct and different patterns. For example, a grandmother may have a very distant and conflicted relationship with her daughter while maintaining a very close relationship with her granddaughter.

One way to think about relationship patterns is to look for reciprocal patterns. A family system is based on maintaining a certain homeostatic balance and these reciprocal relationship patterns help keep this balance in check. For example, if one person in the family is distant, there may be another person who will pursue closeness. Another example is when a person in the family who shows irresponsibility by acting out, not having goals, or by performing poorly (underfunctioning) will be counter-balanced by a family member who is overly responsible for others (overfuntioning). A third example is antagonistic behavior being balanced by excessive pleasing and accommodating behavior.

One of the most important benefits of working with your family genogram is being able to determine what *your* particular relationship patterns are within the family. This is part of *your* emotional process. In other words, it is the relationship pattern you use particularly when you experience increased anxiety. These patterns are deeply ingrained in you and will surface automatically in your relationships with family members

A family system is based on maintaining a certain homeostatic balance. The reciprocal relationship patterns in a family help keep this balance in check.

"Anxiety" is neither good nor bad. It is not equivalent to what we call stress, although it may involve feeling stressed. Anxiety is the normal biological-emotional response we have to situations.

RECIPROCAL
RELATIONSHIP
PATTERNS

Overfunctioning and
Underfunctioning

Pursuit and Flight

Co-dependency

Overdependent and
Underdependent

Strong and Weak

Leader and Follower

Pleasing and
Antagonistic

and others outside the family. It is important to understand how this pattern developed, what the emotional "triggers" are that evoke the behavior and how your patterns differ with each family member. For example, some people become very accommodating and pleasing when mother becomes angry or upset. If this is true of a male in the home you can anticipate how this same patterned response will be triggered if, later, his wife becomes angry and upset.

To help you begin to identify your family emotional process take a look at these patterns and note the one(s) that best describe how you relate to your family members.

Which of these best describes how you relate to others in your family?

- ❏ Fight to the death
- ❏ See no evil, speak no evil
- ❏ Peace at all costs
- ❏ Odd man out
- ❏ I'll never tell – anything!
- ❏ Every man for himself
- ❏ I know the answer to your problems
- ❏ You are the problem, not me
- ❏ If there's trouble, I'm out of here
- ❏ If you feel it, I feel it
- ❏ I'll do anything you want
- ❏ Why does everyone pick on me?
- ❏ Nothing bothers me—really!
- ❏ Two can play at that game
- ❏ Is this o.k. with everyone?
- ❏ I'd rather do it myself
- ❏ That's really none of your business.

Describe your relationship pattern for each of the following persons in your family of origin:

- ▪ Mother
- ▪ Father
- ▪ Siblings
- ▪ Grandparents

- ❏ How does your relationship differ in each?

- ❏ Can you spot a pattern of behavior? Which of these patterns bothers you the most?

- ❏ How do these behaviors affect your functioning?

❑ How do these behaviors affect the functioning of others?

❑ How do these behaviors impact the functioning of the family as a whole?

❑ Are there reciprocal patterns in your relationship with each?

❑ Do you see different patterns emerge when there is a crisis?

Triangles

By diagramming relationship patterns, you can begin to identify the triangles in your family. Triangles are very important in helping to reveal the emotional process in a family system. Triangles are patterns between three family members that are unconsciously formed to maintain a homeostatic balance in family relationships or to handle anxiety between two parties. The basic rule of the triangle is: *when instability or conflict is present between two family members, a third family member will often be pulled in to stabilize or solidify the family relations in general.*

See Appendix A: "The Seven Laws of Emotional Triangles."

Triangles are a normal part of family relationships and no one escapes them. The important triangles to note on your genogram are the ones that become a set pattern with little room for optional behavior. In other words, anxious, patterned triangles are rigid; limiting the choices of those involved, or, even whether or not to be caught in one! You can spot triangles easily because they are repetitive and predictable. One of the most common patterns is when parents triangle one of the children. For example, if a husband is distant from his wife, the wife may compensate by focusing more intensely on one of the children; thus a triangle is formed that may become "set," or a patterned way of relating in the family (see Figure 1). Often the child caught in the parental triangle with the most intensity will display some particular characteristics or "symptoms." These can include acting out (and therefore becoming the Identified Patient as depicted below), being "perfect," unconsciously following in the family "footsteps," or not performing well in life.

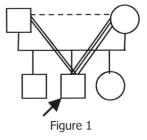

Figure 1

The triangle that exists between you and your parents will begin to tell you the most about your own emotional process. This relationship pattern tends to format how you respond to others in the world. Often this triangle determines what pushes your "hot button" and determines where you have less flexibility in your functioning and in your relationships with others.

Multigenerational Transmission of Patterns

The new bride was making her first dinner for her husband and tries her hand at her mother's roast recipe. The new husband watched puzzled as his bride cut off the ends of the roast, threw them away, and placed the roast in the oven. Not wanting to dampen his wife's enthusiasm at cooking their first meal, he said nothing.

After the meal the husband said, "Honey, that was delicious!" The new bride beamed with joy.

The husband paused, then asked, "Darling, I'm just curious about one thing."

"What is it, my love?" she asked.

"Why did you cut off the ends of the roast and throw them away? That piece of meat was rather expensive."

"Why, that's the way my mother always cooked roast, dear," replied the bride. "It's just how it's done, silly."

At the next visit with his mother-in-law the young husband could not resist asking about the roast. He explained to his mother-in-law about how his bride cut off the ends of the roast before putting it in the oven and asked if she knew what that was about.

The mother-in-law replied, "That's the way my mother always cooked roast. That's just how it's done, sweetie."

At this point the young man's curiosity was piqued. He was sure he was missing something, "There can't be a reason why there's a need to cut off the end of an expensive slab of meat to cook it," he thought to himself. Determined, and at his wit's end, he called the grandmother. He explained his puzzlement at how his wife cooked the roast, how *her* mother cooked the roast in the same way, and their unsatisfactory explanation for why they did it that way.

"So," he asked, "I wonder if you can tell me why you need to cut off the ends of the roast before cooking it," he asked.

The grandmother laughed and said, "Why, the answer is simple! I had a very small oven, and that's the only way the roast would fit in the pan!"

Family patterns tend to repeat themselves within and across the generations. Basic relationship patterns between parents and children are often so ingrained that they may be unconsciously passed down through the generations and will be repeated in future generations. Not only are relationship patterns transmitted intergenerationally, but beliefs, trends, roles, and values are embedded in the family in direct and subtle ways. These can influence the choices you make in partners, the career you choose, the religious practices you observe, the beliefs you hold (whether they are true or not), your prejudices, and, of course, your interactions with people.

Refer to your genogram and try to identify multigenerational patterns, issues, themes, or crises. After you have done so, consider the following:

- Identify the relationship triangles that are repeated in the generations above and below you.

- Have the triangles changed over time?

- Do the triangles skip generations?

- Are certain triangles "mirror images" to your current patterns?

- Are there patterns related to illnesses?

- Are there patterns related to alcohol or drug dependency?

- Are there patterns of abuse, lawlessness, or violence?

- Are there patterns of success and achievement?

- Are there patterns related to religion?

- Are there patterns of cutoff, fights, migrations or, conversely, are there patterns of stability?

- What beliefs, trends and values can you identify in your family system that have influenced you most?

Dates and Nodal Events

Dates and chronology are an important part in understanding the family system. They provide information that helps put events in perspective enhancing the understanding of relationship patterns and clarifying emotional responses in the family. Nodal family events such as deaths, births, divorces, accidents, criminal activities, losses, and crises can create long-lasting patterns or beliefs.

See Appendix B for a timeline worksheet.

Take a look at your genogram to determine when these nodal events occurred. Highlight any simultaneous events such as a birth that occurs soon after the death of a pivotal person in the family or several losses occurring in a short time span. For example, a child born after the death of another child may "inherit" excessive focus or specific family expectations. Note repetitive events such as divorces, early deaths, and illnesses. These may result in specific beliefs or trends in the family. An example of this is a family with a number of early deaths resulting in an attitude of "life is short, so have fun while you can."

Determine if you can correlate a nodal event with emotional responses within the family or changes in family patterns. Sometimes nodal events create a family belief or trend that will repeat itself over the generations. Creating a time line can be very illustrative in identifying how nodal events impact the family's emotional process. These time lines can center on such issues as illnesses, significant losses, divorces, and changes in vocation or economic status.

Examine your genogram, and then consider the following:

❑ What were the nodal events in your family?

❑ How did these events impact the family?

❑ Do you remember how these nodal events shaped your beliefs? Did they change the way you related to family members?

❑ What repeating patterns or beliefs do you see as a result of these events?

Illnesses and Dysfunction

Tracking physical and mental illnesses and dysfunctions like drug and alcohol abuse, obesity, and smoking can provide some insight into family patterns and beliefs. Very often, families will have a repeating pattern of illnesses or dysfunction that impacts family beliefs and functioning. For example, a pattern of alcoholism in the women in the family may create a belief that women are not dependable. An occurrence of incest may influence the beliefs about men in the family, attitudes about sex, or beliefs about safety, trust, and protection. Consider how your family handles illnesses and the attitudes that result from them. Repetition of the same issue through the generations may have a more significant long-range impact on the family than a single occurrence of the illness itself.

Birth Order and Roles

As you look at your family genogram, note the birth order of family members. Birth order in families may dictate particular roles and influence how a family member functions depending on the mutigenerational trends. For example, eldest males may be the ones who are selected to carry on the family legacy or the youngest female may get the job of caring for the parents as they age. A middle child may be expected to be the peacemaker. A youngest male may get the role of the "black sheep" or the (incompetent) "baby" of the family. Roles and expectations related to birth order may vary from family to family although there are universal trends that accompany birth order. Birth order does not only affect sibling relationships, but parenting as well. For

An event is said to be "nodal" when it brings about a change in an individual or a family system—its structure or its emotional process. It is not the event itself that is significant; rather, it's the way the family or a member is affected by it.

Good books on birth order and roles:

Richardson & Richardson, *Birth Order and You* (Self-Counsel Press, 1990)

Toman, *Family Constellation* (Springer Publishing Co., 1993)

example, parents who are both youngest children in their family of origin may have different expectations of their offspring than two oldest parents.

Gender

Gender beliefs and values may thread through families in direct and subtle ways. These beliefs often impact whom we select as a partner, influence our relationships with opposite and same sex family members, inform our attitudes and can create difficulties when we marry someone with different gender beliefs. Consider your family's views of gender roles and correlate that to functioning, relationship patterns and roles.

Blessings and Legacies

One of the best things about families is that they can pass on blessings and legacies generation after generation. Blessings acknowledge our place and worth in the family system. They celebrate our individuality, acknowledge our gifts and talents, and can open up a world of possibilities for us. Blessings affirm that we are a part of the family and often identify a special place that we occupy in the family system: heir, standard-bearer, the emergent patriarch or matriarch, "family chaplain," hero, saint, sage, caregiver, or leader. Legacies come in many forms. Most families pass on legacies related to religious belief and faith, culture, social values, family history and traditions. Some legacies may be monetary or related to a family business. And some legacies can be as simple as objects and artifacts: the family Bible, mother's good china, great-grandmother's quilt, or Dad's coin collection.

Refer to your genogram and recall stories or incidents that can answer the following:

❑ Can you describe how your family celebrates or handles blessings and legacies?

❑ Who in the family tends to receive these?

❑ Are there rites, rituals, events, or ceremonies that center around the blessing or the passing on of a family legacy?

❑ What blessings and legacies from your family do you carry?

Family Secrets

Family secrets or taboo subjects significantly influence the family's emotional process but the impact of these "secrets" are often less evident on the surface. Secrets center on issues of perceived "shame" that in and of themselves aren't necessarily "good" or "bad" but are often seen by the family as negative information that must not be discussed. Among others, secrets might include issues surrounding homosexuality, divorce, incest, incarcerations, financial failures, suicides, criminal activities, economic status, or mental illness. These can profoundly impact family values, beliefs, performance pressure and relationship patterns but they are like hidden agendas. You might have a sense that there is something "going on" but you don't know exactly what it is. Clues might be that you have inexplicable feelings about yourself, pressure to perform in a certain manner that makes no sense, or when you seem to act upon unfounded beliefs. Subjects that are never talked about or avoided in the family are also clues that merit some investigation. These may take longer to discover than other information about the family and require more careful investigative work on your part. Look for unexplained gaps in the family genogram, information that no one seems to know, and topics that people in the family are vague about or won't discuss.

Very often you can find one family member who is willing to talk openly about these family "secrets." Sometimes this is a "playful" person, or a family misfit who does not mind "embarrassing" the family by talking about the elephant in the room (or the skeletons in the closet). Either way, if you can find that person, he or she can be a great source of information!

Other Family Information Affecting Beliefs and Values

There are many other issues that you can explore through your genogram to help you uncover how your family works and to understand your place in it. Here are additional areas and themes to identify and explore in your family genogram:

- ❑ Ethnic or racial background

- ❑ Religion or changes in religious beliefs

- ❑ Education

- ❑ Economic status

- ❑ Military service

❑ Geographic origin or location of family members

❑ Occupations

❑ Political views

❑ Immigration from a foreign country.

    By this point you should have a good idea about how to start interpreting your family genogram. Have some fun thinking about these issues and enjoy meeting with family members to learn things you didn't know about how your family works the way it does, why individuals in the family behave as they do, and how you came to be the way you are! The next chapter in this workbook will help you focus on twenty specific areas concerning your relationship with, and place within, your family.

Chapter 3

The "20 Questions" To Ask
About Your Family

We have always enjoyed the game "20 Questions." You've probably played it. In this game someone thinks about a person, place, or thing, and players get to ask twenty questions to guess what the person is thinking about. If you ask the right questions you can usually arrive at the answer. We were always fascinated at the phenomenon behind that: ask the *right* twenty questions and you can determine what someone else is thinking!

Now that you have created your genogram, and have been introduced to some basic interpretive concepts, it's time to explore some key issues about the emotional system of your family. The following questions will guide you to a deeper exploration of your genogram and what insights it might reveal about your family and yourself. You do not need to answer the questions in order, nor do you need to answer all of them, although you will get the most out of your genogram work if you try. Consider working through these questions with your family members. Often, family members have different perspectives, interpretations, and recollections depending on their birth order, the life cycle of the family at the time of their awareness of a particular experience in the family, and other factors. There is no need to insist on a "right" interpretation of family events or dynamics, since people perceive these from their own position in the system. Allowing for this fact can help provide you with a richer, more nuanced, and multidimensional understanding of your family.

If you find a particular question or issue uncomfortable, or if you find yourself resisting dealing with it, take that as a hint that the question is something important you need to pursue. Often, we initially resist those areas we most need to work on. In such a case, asking another family member the question "How would you answer this question?" can get you unstuck and can provide a new perspective to consider.

1. In what ways did the birth order of the persons in your family affect relationships and functioning?

One consistent family pattern dynamic is that people who grow up in the same sibling position have common and predictable characteristics. These characteristics are not "good" or "bad," but they can set us up for complementary or conflictual ways of relating to others. For example, a boss who is an oldest child may work well with an assistant who is a "youngest" in the family. Youngest children who are bosses may like to be in charge, but their leadership style typically differs from an oldest's style. Additionally, when anxious, they may have difficulty in accepting that they are indeed "the boss."

Birth order, or "sibling position," can influence our relationships with other family members. For instance, the birth orders of spouses can influence how they relate to each other. Additionally, the birth order of parents can influence how they relate to their children and can differ child to child given the birth order of the children.

Describe how your birth order in your family of origin affected your place in the family and the ways you related to your family members.

How did the birth order of your parents affect the way they related to each other and to the children in the family?

How did the birth orders of your siblings affect the ways they functioned in your family? How do you see their birth order affect their own nuclear families now if they are married and have their own children?

How does birth order affect you and your spouse (or partner) and the way you relate to your own children?

BIRTH ORDER:

❑ Only child
❑ First born
❑ Second born
❑ Middle child
❑ Youngest

VARIATIONS TO CONSIDER:

❑ Adopted child and sibling position
❑ Oldest male
❑ Oldest female
❑ Youngest male
❑ Youngest female
❑ Blended families birth orders and sibling position

2. What was your role in the family system?

COMMON FAMILY
ROLES:

The Golden Child
The Scapegoat
The Black Sheep
The Victim
The Hero
The Fixer
The Problem-solver
The Caretaker
The Family Chaplain
The "Glue"
The Godfather
Matriarch or Patriarch
The Elder
The Baby
The Standard Bearer
The Screw up
The Princess
The Peacemaker
The Sick One
The Strong One

*Self-differentiation is the capacity to be one's own true self while staying connected to others in one's family and other relationship systems. It includes knowing your values, being principled, knowing your boundaries and respecting those of others.

Families often "assign" roles to family members although this is not done consciously, for the most part. Often roles are assigned of necessity, by default, because of birth order, or as a way to ensure that a certain function is provided to the family as a whole. Sometimes family roles are chosen by individuals in the family as a way to self-differentiate* from, or within, the family.

Identify your role in your family of origin. What purpose or function did it serve for your larger family? Do you play the same role in other relationship systems in your life (your work system, your church, your current family)?

What were the roles of the other persons in your family of origin? How did their role affect the family? How did it affect you?

3. Who carried the legacy in the family system? Who is the standard bearer?

Multigenerational transmission describes the process of how the levels of emotional maturity (differentiation) between parents (or founders, matriarchs and patriarchs in a system) and their offspring are passed down generation to generation. These differences are transmitted across generations through relationships and events and can happen on several interconnected levels; from the conscious teaching and learning of information to the automatic and unconscious programming of emotional reactions and behaviors. Commonly, this transmitted information (through relationship patterns or even genetically) interacts to shape both the family system and the persons who make it up. The power of these multigenerational patterns can be greatly underappreciated unless we make an intentional effort to understand them, or, in the case of the unconscious variety, to discover them.

One example of multigenerational transmission is how families choose the "standard bearer." Often first-born standard bearers receive a "family blessing" (which means that sometimes another person in the family does not). But a blessing can also be a burden, something that firstborns intuitively understand given the expectations that often come with that sibling position; from carrying on the family business (from a shop to a corporation to becoming a clergy), to ensuring the survival of the family name, to carrying on a family role.

Using your genogram identify the standard bearers in your family system. Are you one of the standard bearers? If not, why not?

Where you named after someone in your extended family? Who? What was the reason that you received that person's name? What does it mean to you?

The biblical story of Jacob and Esau is a classic family legacy-blessing story. You can read this story, which has universal family themes, in Genesis chapters 27 and 28.

4. What assumptions about gender did your family of origin have?

Gender "roles" and gender "functions" are not always equivalent. For example, the roles of "breadwinner" or "disciplinarian" can be assumed by a family member of either gender. But only a female can function as "Mom," and only a male can function as "Father." In other words, culture does not trump biology in terms of emotional process.

While culture does not trump biology a family's beliefs about the sexes can influence self-understanding, roles, and relationships. Beliefs and values about gender may be communicated through families in powerful yet subtle ways; creating difficulties when a member marries someone with different gender beliefs, when an ethnic family moves out of its cultural context, or when a "generation gap" develops between older and younger generations. For example, if you discover that your family has sent clear messages that men are strong and do not show emotions, you may come to understand why a certain younger generation husband and wife in your family system are struggling in their marriage.

What were the expectations or beliefs about males in your family of origin?

What were the expectations and beliefs about females in your family?

Have these expectations, values and beliefs changed for you? In what ways? How did that come about?

5. Does your family system have an "illness of choice"?
What is it?

Chronic illnesses, or instances of acute illness, often shape or shift family emotional process. Some families develop patterns of chronic illnesses due to genetics, and/or others due to emotional process. These patterned illnesses are sometimes called an "illness of choice." Examine your genogram and determine whether you can identify an "illness of choice" in the family system that is present in three or more generations of your family.

Is there an illness of choice in your family system? Is it genetic? Is it the result of emotional process or psychological factors?

How has this illness of choice affected individual family members?

How has this illness of choice affected the multigenerational family system? In what ways does the illness of choice show up as a pattern?

EXAMPLES OF ILLNESSES THAT CAN BECOME PATTERNED "ILLNESSES OF CHOICE"

- Alcoholism
- Diabetes
- Obesity
- Genetic disorders
- Mental Illness
- Phobias
- Dementia (Alzheimer's)
- Cancer
- Heart disease
- Drug abuse
- Chemical dependency
- Addictions (gambling, sex)
- Physical, mental, or sexual abuse

ON THE POSITIVE SIDE

Some families are blessed with what can be considered above-average traits: physical athleticism or mental acuity for example. Do you have a family of athletes or a family of geniuses? A musically talented family? Explore those gifts and talents that are prominent in your family system.

6. Chose the "family theme" or motto that comes closest to describing your family of origin. If none match, then name the "family theme" or motto of your system (or, you can choose a "theme song" for your family).

- ❑ "Peace at any price."
- ❑ "All for one and one for all."
- ❑ "Us against the world."
- ❑ "We are the perfect family."
- ❑ "What happens in Vegas stays in Vegas."
- ❑ "Father knows best."
- ❑ "Mom wears the pants in the family."
- ❑ "Too many cooks in the kitchen."
- ❑ "Too many braves, not enough chiefs."
- ❑ "The family that prays together stays together."
- ❑ "Don't tread on me."
- ❑ "I've got a secret."
- ❑ "Let's you and him/her fight."
- ❑ "You're not the boss of me."
- ❑ "Walking on eggshells."
- ❑ "I hear you knocking but you can't come in."
- ❑ "Lost in space."
- ❑ "The family that plays together stays together."
- ❑ "Friday Night Fights."
- ❑ "Home Sweet Home"
- ❑ "Publicize our successes; hide our failures"

Share a few stories or recall some incidents that illustrate your family theme.

Does your family theme or motto continue in your life? In your current family? In what ways? Give an example.

7. How was anger expressed in your family of origin?

Anger is not merely a feeling, it is a form of "emotional functioning" that affects relationships and emotional process in the family. Anger is "transactional," meaning, that how people deal with anger creates a mutual impact on each other. Your family members were affecting others, and being affected, by the ways in which anger was handled (avoiding, denying, expressing or suppressing it) in the family. How you learned to deal with anger in your family of origin taught you a lot about how to relate to other persons and how to handle your own emotions, and theirs.

Who in your family made you most angry or upset? How did you cope with your anger?

Did anger in your family lead to a cut-off, depression, or violence? Give an example.

COMMON COPING POSTURES FOR ANGER

- ❑ Avoid dealing with it
- ❑ Deny that one is angry
- ❑ Express one's anger
- ❑ Suppress one's anger

8. How was love expressed and communicated in your family?

The ways that a family expresses and communicates affection, intimacy, and love says a lot about its emotional state. These ways can hint at how patterns of relationship get formed and are perpetuated. One of the most important relationship patterns in families has to do with the together-separateness dynamics. The extreme togetherness dynamic can be a form of enmeshment, while the extreme form of separateness can be a kind of distancing or a cutoff.

Plot your family of origin's way of expressing love on the continuum below, then share a story or incident that illustrates why you plotted your family so.

INTIMATE ⟵————————————⟶ DISTANT

Plot your family of origin's way of communicating love on the continuum below. Give a few examples about how your family communicated "I love you."

THROUGH WORDS ⟵————————⟶ THROUGH ACTIONS

How do you communicate and demonstrate love in your own family? In your relationships? Have you learned to do so differently over the years? From whom did you learn this?

9. What were you like in your family of origin when you were around 10 years old?

About the age of 10 or so, most children experience a "coming of age." They are able for the first time to experience and become aware of dynamics in the family that previously were inaccessible. For example, they are able to distinguish their parents by gender and role (Dad is a male who is married to a woman. He is a husband and a father. Mom is a female who is married to a man. She is a wife and a mother). Consequently, children have to work at their place in the family and on their relationship with family members in new ways. Children also begin to learn and think about what it means to be a male or female, and about expectations related to gender. Sometimes it makes a difference where our family was in its family life cycle when we turned 10. The impact on a child of a nodal event, such as an illness, a death, a move, or the divorce of parents can be greatly amplified if it occurs around age 10. It is therefore helpful to think back to the time when we were that age for important clues about our family emotional process and our own personal functioning.

What was your relationship to each of your parents when you were 10 years old? Describe it.

What major family events can you recall when you were about 10 years old? How did your family handle these events? How do you remember feeling about them?

If you could go back in time and visit yourself, what would you like to tell yourself as a 10 year old?

COMING OF AGE:

Coming of age is a popular theme in literature and film. Consider how may stories there are about children between the ages of 10 and 13. Here are just a few:

<u>NOVELS</u>

Johnny Tremain
The Adventures of Huckleberry Finn
Tom Sawyer
Shane
Treasure Island
A Tree Grows in Brooklyn
Madeleine
David Copperfield
Great Expectations
A Wrinkle in Time
Dandelion Wine
Something Wicked This Way Comes
The Yearling
How Green Was My Valley
The Black Stallion
Angela's Ashes
To Kill A Mockingbird
The Red Pony
Oliver Twist
The Golden Compass
Lord of the Flies

<u>MOVIES</u>

The Harry Potter series
National Velvet
The Road to Perdition
The Sandlot
Flight of the Navigator
Seabiscuit
Unbreakable
Stand By Me

10. What was your perception of your parent's relationship when you were growing up?

The primary relationship in the family is the adult marital relationship. This primary relationship "sets the tone" for the family emotional process, can foster and perpetuate triangles, and can facilitate or impede the emotional health of the family and its members. Understanding the nature and workings of the parental relationship in your family of origin can give you insight into many of the things that made your family what it was, and influenced you in ways that shaped the person you have become.

What was your parents' relationship like? Intimate? Conflictual? Distant? Affectionate?

Was one of your parents the "leader" in the home? Which one? Describe how that worked in the family.

Growing up, what was the relationship like between your parents and your siblings? Did your parents favor one sibling over the other? Did they overfocus on one?

What did you learn about parenting from your parents that you carry with you today in your own parenting and/or relationships with others?

FOUR BASIC FACTORS IN FAMILY RELATION-SHIP PATTERNS:

- Marital conflict
- Dysfunction in one spouse
- Impairment in one or more children
- Emotional distance.

11. Where do you see the major triangles in your family of origin?

Triangles that are formed through the relationship of three family members are very important in family systems theory and the analysis of genograms. In fact, you should spend a lot of time discovering where your family triangles exist and how they came about. These triangles represent a particular kind of relationship that can have both positive and negative effects on the family as a system. Triangles are neither "good" nor "bad," they are just a way to handle anxiety in relationships. One of the basic principles of family systems theory is that the family system will naturally seek homeostasis (a balance of what feels "normal") or some type of balance. When instability or conflict is present between two family members, a third family member will often be pulled in to stabilize the family relations in an effort to achieve homeostasis.

Can you identify the major triangles in your family of origin? Who were the players and what was the triangle about?

What triangles where you a part of in your family of origin? What triangles are you currently a part of (in your family or in your workplace)?

Often, there exists a major triangle in the family system. These major triangles tend to be the origin of interlocking triangles. Can you identify the major triangle in your family genogram?

Refer to Appendix A: "Seven Laws of an Emotional Triangle" when answering these questions.

A TRIANGLE is a three-person (or two persons and an issue) relationship system. Triangles are the building blocks of larger emotional systems because they make for a more stable relationship system. A two-person system is unstable and impossible to maintain so it will not take long, or much, for it to involve a third person (or an issue). A triangle can contain much more tension (anxiety) because the tension can shift around three relation-ships. If the tension is too high for one triangle to handle, it will create a series of "interlocking" triangles.

12. Can you identify cutoffs in your family genogram?

Cutoff does not primarily involve geographic distance, even though some people physically move away from their families and rarely visit home as a way to deal with unresolved issues. But a cutoff can also happen by people staying in physical contact with their families but avoiding communication, being emotionally "absent" or generally avoiding each other (locking oneself up in one's room, not eating together as a family, etc.). Sometimes this kind of cutoff feels like "walking on eggshells" in the family.

The concept of emotional cut-off refers to a way of managing unresolved emotional issues with others (parents, siblings, other family members and other relationships) by reducing or attempting to totally cut off emotional contact with them. As a rule emotional cutoff is a poor way to manage anxiety and issues since the problems remain dormant and unresolved. Some family systems develop a pattern of cutoff behavior.

Examine your genogram. Can you spot cutoffs? Is cutoff a pattern in your family for how people deal with poor relationships? With stress or anxiety? With crisis?

Who paid the price for cutoffs in your family system? Was that price paid willingly or unwillingly?

Was the cutoff a blessing or a curse?

13. In what ways do you see learned patterns of behavior (the ways you behave) in your family system playing out in your work system?

Family emotional process shapes our patterns of relationships. We often learn to relate to people, and to cope with issues and feelings, in a non-thinking, reactive manner that is a result of how we learned to relate to others. We bring these patterns of relating to other people with us into other relationship systems outside of our family: school, work, church, marriage, even a sports team, etc.

How are the ways in which you functioned in your family system playing out now in your relationships with friends, groups, or your work system?

In what ways has your family system shaped you to do the work you've chosen? Or, do you feel that, given your family background, you've "missed your calling"?

COMMON RECIPROCAL FUNCTIONING:

Related to birth order: people act out their family role in their workplace system (peacemaker, oldest, "baby," the helper, etc.)

Related to overfunctioning: people who overfunction at home tend to do the same at work. Paradoxically, in some cases people overfunction in certain ways at work, yet underfunction in other ways at home.

14. What is the ethnic background or heritage of your family of origin?

Your family's ethnicity can be a powerful influence because ethnic values and identification are retained for many generations after immigration despite assimilation into a "new" culture. Ethnic or cultural family issues may be reflected in views regarding age, gender, family and life roles, expressiveness, birth order, separation, status, etc. For example, a cultural patriarchy might frown upon a women who chooses a career path that takes her outside its normal and accepted roles for women. This could lead to cut-off or "black sheep" identification among other reactions. An examination of a genogram might reveal this type of dynamic in the current or previous generations or both.

Studying your genogram, can you identify the ways your ethnic heritage affects how your family members relate to each other? Describe those ways.

Are there particular and distinct family values associated with your ethnic heritage that continue to influence your family and/or its members?

Are there distinct cultural practices and customs that your family continues to observe? Are there some that your family has ceased to observe? Tell about those.

15. Can you identify an overfunction/underfunction reciprocity dynamic in your family of origin? In your current family?

Overfunctioning and underfunctioning are reciprocal functions; that is, you can't have one without the other. Overfunctioning happens when someone takes responsibility for what rightly belongs to another person. Overfunctioning, no matter how right it feels to the overfunctioner, always is invasive of another person's boundaries.

Looking at your genogram, can you identify any overfunctioners in your family system? Who are they? In what ways do they overfunction?

Who are the underfunctioners in the family? Describe the ways they underfunction. Who reciprocates by overfunctioning for them? How?

Are you an overfunctioner or an underfunctioner? In what areas? Describe how you feel when you do either. Who in your family reciprocates?

16. How did your family handle crises?

Most family crises result in some level of acute anxiety. Interestingly, it seems to be a family's ability to tap into its resources, rather than the level of anxiety, issue, or type of crisis, that is the determinative factor in how well families handle anxiety.

A family's capacity to handle crises is indicative of, and dependent upon, many factors related to emotional process. The healthier the family, the more resilient it can be when faced with a crisis. Healthy families have within them the resources to regain homeostasis or to adapt to new and challenging circumstances. Families that do not handle crises well can get stuck, engage in blaming or scapegoating, spawn new triangles, feel victimized and powerless, and can be done in by even minor crises.

Review your genogram as you respond to the following questions. Diagram the emotional process dynamics (for example, triangles) to illustrate your insight.

Can you remember a time when your family had to deal with a crisis? Describe how your family dealt with it. Were the members highly reactive or did they cope well? Was the primary posture "fight" or "flight"?

Looking at your genogram, who are the members of your family (past or present) that responded to crisis well? What strengths do they possess that allowed a positive response from them? Do you see patterns in your genogram that tend to identify this type of person?

Looking at your genogram, who are the members of your family that responded to crisis poorly? Why do you think they responded this way? Do you see patterns in your genogram that tend to identify this type of person?

Can you identify the things or issues that tend to throw your family into crisis mode or make them anxious? Money issues? Health issues? Children's behaviors? Religion? Alcohol or drug abuse? A parent's behavior?

When a crisis happens in your family what triangles get formed? Are roles assigned?

17. What is the role and function of spirituality, faith or religion in your family?

Religion and faith are important dimensions of family life because, at heart, these form core values and teach us how to relate to others. In addition religion and faith address the question of meaning and purpose of our lives on earth. Even an absence of attention to family religious practices can have an influence in a family. A "religious practice" may be formal or informal, faith-oriented or culture (ethnic)-oriented, or it may be a regular devotional practice.

My family then....

1. *What is your memory of your family's religious practices when you were growing up? Did you have unique cultural observances? Did you observe a religious family tradition? Do you remember a family devotional experience that was very meaningful to you?*

2. *Describe your memories about your family church or faith community experience when you were about 10 years old. If your family did not attend church, share what you remember about your family's faith, beliefs, or experiences with religion.*

3. *On your genogram, identify the most religious person in your family system. Who were the "saints" and who were the sinners in your family system? Identify them on your genogram.*

My family now...

4. *Describe the religious and devotional practices that your family currently observes. Are there some that individual family members observe and some that the family observes as a whole? Explain those.*

5. *Name some "religious artifacts" that you have at home (pictures, paintings, art, objects, heirlooms, icons, etc.). Are these merely decorative objects, or do they have a meaning for you and your family? For an individual family member? Share about that.*

18. At what point in your family's lifecycle were you born? At what point did you "leave home"?

THE FAMILY LIFE CYCLE:

1. **Pre-marital Stage** (courtship, planning)
2. **Establishing Stage** (up to seven years, with or without children)
3. **Parenting Stage** (birth of first born)
4. **Early Family Stage** (becoming a family. Birth of siblings)
5. **Later Family Stage** (oldest child a teenager)
6. **Launching Stage** (oldest child in college or leaves home. Other children preparing to leave.) This stage may extend as adult children return to live at home after college before they get established on their own.
7. **Empty Nest Stage** (all children gone from home)
8. **Generational Stage** (parents become grandparents)

Events that can abort or change the trajectory of the normal family life cycle include divorce, family dissolution, deaths, tragedies and events (wars, migration), couples with no children, etc.

Families are not static. They grow, change, evolve, and go through generally predictable life cycles of development. The point in a family life cycle we made our appearance, through birth or adoption or as part of a blended family, can make a big difference in family relationships and structures. It is not uncommon for siblings to experience family in very different ways depending on what stage of the family life cycle they were born into. For these questions refer to the dates on your genogram.

Can you identify the point in your family's life cycle you were born into?

Growing up, what life cycle stage do you most remember of your family? At what family stage did you "come of age" (ages 10-13)?

At what life cycle stage did you leave your family? What was the occasion of your leaving? Natural and developmental, like going off to college? A cutoff? Expulsion? Because of a crisis?

Where any of your siblings born into the family at a different life cycle stage than you? How did their experience of the family differ from yours?

Does your genogram reveal any patterns related to a particular life cycle. For example, do the oldest children seem to leave home in a cut-off fashion? With a blessing? Do marriages seem to have trouble during the empty nest stage? Do divorces happen early in the marriage?

19. How did your family handle losses?

A key genogram factor for understanding the emotional process of your family is the issue of losses. There are many kinds of losses (losses due to critical illness, death, disabilities, economic reversals, job losses, miscarriages, divorces, loss of a home, or a heritage, etc.). The experience of such losses and the depth of pain people feel vary, but all losses involve mourning and grieving. Mourning is the external actions, customs, rituals, and expressions associated with a loss. Grieving is the internal emotional processes associated with loss: depression, sadness, loss of hope, anger, reconciliation, etc.

How did your family express mourning for a loss? Tell a story that illustrates how your family, or individuals in your family, mourned the loss of a person either through death or another kind of loss.

How did your family members handle grief? Sometimes individuals in the same family handle grief differently. Was that true of your own family?

What were the most significant deaths in your family? How did the death of that person affect the family? Was there a conflict? Was there a shift in family responsibilities as a result?

Looking at your genogram, do you see a shift in functioning for certain family members as a result of a loss?

A DEATH IN THE FAMILY AS A NODAL EVENT

Sometimes the death of a significant person in the family becomes a "nodal event." A nodal event is one that causes a shift in the family, a reorganization, a breach, or a shift in function among the family members. For example, a death that is a nodal event can heal a cut-off in some families, but it can cause one in another.

20. Does your family have a skeleton in the closet?

Family secrets are an impediment to healthy family emotional process. A family secret can be something truly hidden from family members or can be an "open secret" that is just not talked about. In either case, communication is stunted and a hierarchy is created consisting of those who know and those who don't. Family "secrets" are not merely individual issues, like a bad habit secretly nursed or a one-time mistake by an individual that is kept hidden. Rather, family secrets are corporate—an event, behavior, pattern, or incident that affects the family system as a whole and therefore has consequences in terms of emotional process. Those in the know are constantly "on guard" to avoid saying anything that touches on the taboo subject. Those "out of the loop" are often running up against unexplained anxiety and avoidance postures from other family members. In the family emotional process, *the fact that there is a secret has far more impact than the actual content of the secret.* Secrets tend to raise the anxiety level of families, not lower them, even when the motive is to "spare" another the pain of knowing the truth. After a secret is revealed, there may be some pain at first but this is usually followed by a lower level of anxiety for the family since everyone now knows the whole story and the entire family can openly learn to deal with and accept what was previously binding, or perpetuating, anxiety. For example, as a rule, children are resilient enough to handle the truth about what's going on in the family, more than they can handle the anxieties surrounding "family secrets."

In studying your genogram do you notice any gaps in information? Are there things your family "does not talk about"? (For example, an unexplained or curious death, vagueness surrounding the reasons for a cut-off; or a resistance to talking about a particular person; or a person whose name or date of death/birth is unknown?).

Are you a family member "in the know" regarding a family secret? What is the secret? Why are you in the loop? Why are others not in the loop?

Chapter 4

Working with Your Family Genogram

At this point you should have a three generation diagram of your family with relevant dates of birth, death and marriage and possibly additional historical content such as vocations, illnesses and nodal events. As you prepared your diagram, some obvious emotional relationship patterns in your family might have already become evident. In addition, your own emotional patterns of relating to others and how those patterns were originally formatted may have started to surface. For the most comprehensive picture of your family's emotional process, continue working until you have a family diagram of at least five generations. This depth is important because some patterns are not easily recognized in a two or three generation diagram.

Genograms require time and patience. It's not uncommon for genogram work to last several years while the process of uncovering more information slowly reveals deeply embedded relationship patterns. Think of it as a "research project" that invites objectivity—a stepping back from the emotional environment to better see how you came to be the way you are. As you continue to evaluate and gather more information, the nuances of your family's emotional process will become clearer. The "pay-off" of genogram work is a better understanding of yourself and your family. The bonus is that it paves the way for greater emotional maturity in the generations that come after you.

In this chapter, we will review techniques for gathering more family information and provide some tips for beginning the challenging work of shifting emotional patterns that inhibit your optimum functioning.

Gathering Family Information

"Why?" questions often go to motive, and questioning people's motives tends to not be very helpful. Additionally, most of us don't have enough insight into our own emotional process to be able to discern "why" we do things (especially when we are anxious or reactive!). Observing *function* is more helpful than trying to determine motives when it comes to figuring out what is going on in a family system.

Take a look at your family genogram to determine where there are gaps in the information you already have. You may begin to close these gaps by talking to peripheral members such as aunts, uncles and cousins. Sometimes it's easier to talk to the family members farther removed from you before talking to the persons closer to you such as parents, siblings and grandparents. Learn all the facts you can by emphasizing who, what, when, where and how—but not *why*. Asking *why* questions open the door for to entanglement in content and motives, rather than facts and emotional process. As you gather information, try to talk to as many family members one-on-one as possible. When spending time with family in group settings, the patterned ways of functioning that maintain homeostatic balance will be more pronounced, and, you will automatically be drawn into these patterns. By talking with each person individually you are less likely to become "stuck" in the emotional process. However, when you are in a family group setting be an astute observer of the patterns that emerge. Notice what happens. Try to imagine "stepping outside yourself" to watch yourself and others interact. Some things to look for include:

Family gatherings like reunions, weddings, and funerals make for an ideal "laboratory" for observing family emotional process in action

- ❑ Who is the dominant person in the group or who demands the most attention?
- ❑ How do other family members respond to the dominant person?
- ❑ Who is the most dependent and "weakest" person who demands attention of another kind?
- ❑ Who gets upset and what triggers their displeasure or distress?
- ❑ How do different family members respond to the person who is upset?
- ❑ What happens to you emotionally?
- ❑ What coalitions are formed?
- ❑ What are the triangles?
- ❑ What is your place in the triangles?
- ❑ What do family stories tell you about myths, rules, expectations, and norms?

Making contact

Make a plan for contacting each family member. Consider the timing of contacts and the questions you want to ask each person. Writing letters or e-mailing can be a good start especially with those who are far away, or with whom you have had little contact. It's also an excellent way to introduce more sensitive issues as writing creates some emotional distance. A written communication can then be followed with a personal visit or phone call. It's particularly important to talk to each parent and sibling alone when addressing issues that are sensitive or emotional in nature. You will get more information this way, and you will be less likely to get caught in the family emotional patterns.

Take the initiative for calling, writing and visiting. Be respectful of the other person's time and be alert to moments when the discussion is becoming too emotional. When this happens, it's wise to stop and continue at a later time. Plan your questions, beginning with the least emotional issues first—such as history and factual data. More emotional issues can be addressed as the comfort level increases over time. For example, when a daughter first asked her mother about their family, the mother answered a few questions and then asked in an anxious, defensive voice, "Why are you asking me all these questions, anyway?" However, the daughter remained gently persistent and, over time, the mother grew more interested and curious herself and began to open up. Asking questions may increase anxiety in the family depending on the level of openness in the family or the sensitivity of issues. In one case, a woman contacting all her aunts and uncles for information but getting "stonewalled" was eventually told that the word among the family was "Don't give her any information. She's writing a book about all the family secrets!" Be patient, ask more than once, ask in a different way, or ask someone else! Be sure to contact everyone—even the family members who seem the most unlikely to know anything or have the least credibility. You may be surprised by what they know! Remember to be as open and unbiased as possible when talking with others. The objective here is to get information, understand perspectives, and identify emotional patterns—*not to get drawn into taking sides or blaming.*

Cut-off Family Members

Cut-offs in families usually have some "reason" that seemingly "explains" the distancing behavior. These distancing behaviors can range from not speaking at all, perhaps for years, to simply being emotionally unavailable. Physical distance is not always a factor but certainly can be. In Family Systems thinking, all cut-offs or distancing behaviors are a way of managing emotional intensity in the family. It's important to contact family members that have been "cut-off" from the family. In most families, there are stories surrounding the reasons for the "cut-off" and definite opinions regarding the person(s) who is "outside" the family circle. Often "cut-off" family members are considered to be family rule

You can use the "20 Questions" handout in Appendix C to interview family members for your genogram. Consider adding your own questions, like:

- How would you describe the relationship between mother/father; grandmother/grandfather, etc.?

- What was it like for you growing up in this family?

- What happened after the death, divorce, (other nodal event)? Who was most affected by it and how? What was it like for you?

- Who did mother/father focus on the most?

When discerning the emotional process in a family through interviews it is often helpful to distinguish "reason" from "cause." *Reasons* are used by people to explain what happened—sometimes in the form of a family myth or by ascribing motive. These reasons may have little to do with the actual *cause* of a cut-off, incident, or behavior. Ask questions that will help you go beyond the *reasons* people give and move you toward the emotional process dynamics that are the *cause.*

breakers or ones whose differences can't be tolerated. It is well worth your time to get to know these family members and form your own opinion about them. Their view of the situation will add perspective to the facts, and this may shed new light on the established "family story." Contacting a "cut-off" member of the family may disturb the homeostasis of the family system especially if the cut-off has been long term and/or antagonistic. Be prepared for this and try to remain calm and playful in the midst of any negative responses you get after making the contact.

Playfulness can help avoid the trap of established family patterns. Being playful is different from joke-telling or delivering witty one-liners. It is "acting" in another way, even opposite, to the usual behavior that may be comfortable or expected of you. The goal is never to change other family members. Instead, being playful helps shift your thinking and lessen your own anxiety.

Using Other Resources

Sometimes you can hit a "brick wall" when information you want is not available because key family members are deceased or there is historical data missing from several generations above you. You may need to resort to other sources for this information. These may include:

- ❑ Visiting cemeteries where family members are interred
- ❑ Researching public records such as census data, birth and death records
- ❑ Old hospital records
- ❑ Real estate deeds and land grants
- ❑ Talking to friends of deceased relatives
- ❑ Church records
- ❑ Wills
- ❑ Old family letters
- ❑ Visiting original "homeplaces" (towns or homesteads)
- ❑ Researching historical markers and correlating them to dates on your genogram (for example, does the Civil War or migrations correspond to major economic changes in the family?)

The Goal of Genogram Work

Perhaps by now, you're wondering just how you are going to use all this family information that you are gathering. How do you go about making it work for you in a productive way? Ultimately, what is its purpose?

The goal is always to work on oneself—not to attempt to "straighten out the family"! In Family System's language this means becoming more of a *self*. In other words, it is striving to function in a more *self-differentiated* manner. This means knowing that your goals and values come from within you as opposed to being influenced by unconscious family patterns, myths and beliefs. An example is the person who chose to be a lawyer because he is the first-born and all first-born children in his family become lawyers. In reality, however, his heart's desire is to become a carpenter. The opposite can also be true—that person can refuse to become a lawyer out of a sense of rebellion. Neither posture comes from within his true *self*.

Being a self-differentiated person also means having the capacity to remain calm and objective especially when others are emotionally reactive. Another important part of being self-differentiated means remaining in relationship with all family members even when the environment is highly charged with emotion and there is pressure either from within you or from others to be emotionally reactive. Studying your genogram can help you to recognize what makes you emotionally reactive and when the family emotional process is in the *"driver's seat"* of your life. This will allow you to make changes in your functioning and ultimately enhance your life. Understanding how patterns of relationship and reactivity developed in the family is helpful because the focus becomes less personal. For example, Anne (see diagram 2) was frequently annoyed by her overbearing mother. From her genogram she discovered that her mother grew up with a critical, domineering mother and that this grandmother experienced the same thing from *her* mother. In addition, Anne's great-grandmother always criticized Anne's grandmother when she came for a visit. When this pattern emerged for Anne she was able to see the issue as less about her and more about her family emotional process. It then became easier for Anne to change her response to her mother.

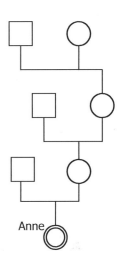

How would you depict the emotional process described in the example on this genogram?

Diagram 2

Self-Differentiating Moves

Working on your own emotional process is a good place to start working on being a more mature, differentiated self. It will help you to identify your hot buttons, how you tend to react to them, and how to choose a different response. A good way to approach this is to function in a way that is opposite to your normal response pattern. Take the case of Anne and her criticizing mother. If Anne's automatic response is to become defensive and angry, she can begin to respond differently by becoming more playful. For example, Anne can ask her mother to write down everything that is wrong so Mom can give her the "list" at the end of the visit.

On the other hand, if you are the overfunctioner and are quick to set people straight about what they should do, then consider playing "dumb." Avoid giving advice. Pretend incompetence and don't volunteer to help or offer an opinion about what you think is the appropriate thing to do. Another example is a parent who constantly pursues a child that is spending lots of time alone in her room. In this situation the parent might commit to refocusing on his or her own activities while ending pleas to the child to spend more time with the family. The parent might even encourage the child to spend *more* time in her room!

The object here is not the functioning of the other person, but rather your own functioning. The golden rule of Family Systems thinking is: "You can only be responsible for yourself and your own functioning." You can never **will** another person to change. In fact, when trying to change someone else, either overtly or indirectly, the result will usually be the opposite of one's intent. Willfulness tends to reinforce the very behaviors that you would like to change in others. When making a self-differentiating move, it is helpful to plan ahead how you will function, what you will say and what kind of response you are likely to get. This planning is beneficial because you will often be caught in the emotional pattern and will revert to your automatic responses. Planning in advance gives you the opportunity to choose your responses to anticipated criticism, resistance, or reactivity.

A good place to focus when working on your self-differentiation is on the primary triangle between you and your parents. This powerful triangle formats many of your unconscious responses to your spouse, children, friends and co-workers. Consider how you can begin to reposition yourself in that parental triangle. For example if you are not close to your father, begin to move toward him. Have more conversations with him, express your thoughts to him, take him out to lunch. If you are in conflict with your mother, work to understand how that came to be, use more playful responses, don't engage in arguments, take her to lunch, or talk more to your grandmother. The goal is to become more mature in your relationship with both parents and with *each* as a separate individual. You will know that you are succeeding when you don't favor one over the other, are less reactive, don't "take sides," and you can relate equally to both.

Tips for Making Self-Differentiated Moves

Here are additional ways to work on making self-differentiating moves:

Take the "I" position. This means speaking for yourself about what you think, want, will do (or won't do) as opposed to blaming, criticizing and speaking for others. Use phrases such as "I believe…" and "I think…." Taking the "I" position can help you manage triangles.

Take responsibility for your own feelings. No one "makes" you feel anything. Your feelings are your own, and you are responsible for the thoughts and actions that are precipitated by those feelings.

Control your own emotional reactivity. When you have identified the "hot buttons" that cause you to become emotionally reactive, you will be able to more easily control your responses. Be flexible in your ability to move between humor and seriousness. Humor, recognition of the absurd and paradox, can be helpful in detoxifying emotional situations. Sometimes it's helpful to think about doing the opposite of what you normally do when these triggers occur. Use feelings as "pointers" for the actions you want to take. Rather than expressing the feelings you have in a reactive way, consider what the feeling is and what action you want to take. Use your thinking capacities to decide how you want to function

Attend all family events such as funerals, birthday celebrations, reunions, anniversary celebrations; etc. This serves three purposes: (1) you will be in a position to connect with family members that you don't ordinarily see, (2) family patterns become more evident, and, (3) you will be able gather more information through family stories in a setting that feels natural for that.

Use times of crises as opportunities to observe family patterns and to make changes in your functioning. Family emotional processes and structures often realign after a significant loss in the family because homeostatic balance shifts to fill the void. When this happens a self-differentiated person can *choose* how to reposition in the family.

Find ways to communicate clearly and openly about matters that are never or rarely talked about in the family. Secrets are often withheld or selectively shared, forming a boundary between the secret holder and the unaware family member. These secret-keeping postures can perpetuate mystification and foster cut-offs.

Managing Sabotage

Most attempts at making a change in your functioning (self-differentiating moves) will upset the family system homeostasis and will likely result in some form of reactivity. Count on this! This is the system's

MANAGING YOURSELF IN TRIANGLES:

- ❑ Insist on one-to-one communication
- ❑ Avoid taking sides
- ❑ Avoid listening to criticism about another person
- ❑ Don't keep "secrets" or accept information "in confidence"
- ❑ Move toward those with whom you are distant
- ❑ Stay connected to the other parties of the triangle
- ❑ Take responsibility for what belongs to you and not for others'

Chapter Four •

"You've changed."

"Turn back, or else."

"You're hurting the family."

"You are betraying us."

"You're wrong."

"You will fail."

"I liked you better before."

"Who do you think you are?"

"You're alone on this."

way of regaining the balance it is most comfortable with and knows best. This reactivity is called sabotage in systems terms. In other words, "No good deed goes unpunished!" Sabotage comes in many forms—seduction, criticism, resistance, or conflict; which serves as a good reminder that often it is not the *content* that counts, but the *function* that a particular behavior serves. Seduction and criticism may feel different, but either one will serve the purpose of getting you off track and pulling you back into homeostasis.

It is important to "keep on, keeping on" in the face of sabotage. If you can stay the course by remaining calm and purposeful in your efforts to self-differentiate, the system may realign itself as family members begin to accept these new changes in your functioning. It's even possible that other family members may begin to make self-differentiating moves. Regardless, you will enjoy a sense of empowerment, become clearer about your personal objectives, experience more energy for doing the things that bring you pleasure, and enhance relationships with all family members.

Using a Coach

Understanding yourself, your family of origin and navigating the changes you want to make are difficult and complex tasks but they are well worth the effort. However, because most of us are so entrenched in our own family emotional process, we can't always see the "forest for the trees." For this reason, it's important to utilize the help of a "coach" in the form of a group, a therapist, a minister, or a colleague. Coaches can often see things that we are unable to see ourselves. They can help us make a plan for self-differentiating moves, assist in recognizing how our reactivity relates to our family of origin, facilitate change and provide encouragement.

We hope that this workbook is the beginning in a lifelong journey toward growth and self-understanding for you and your family. We want to encourage you to continue to work on your genogram and on your own personal maturity and health through study, staying connected to your family in deeper honest relationships, and, by working on your self-differentiation. Our families shape us, and we become the person we are as a result. But we too can shape our families by virtue of our own choices and our influence. We hope you'll choose the best for yourself and your family!

Seven Laws of an Emotional Triangle

1. The relationship of any two persons in an emotional triangle is kept in balance by the way a third person relates to each of them or to their relationship.

2. Attempts to change the relationship of the other two sides of an emotional triangle not only are generally ineffective, but also, the opposite of one's intent tends to happen.

3. To the extent a third person in an emotional triangle tries to change the relationship of the other two, the more likely it is that the third person will wind up with the stress for the other two.

4. The various triangles in an emotional system interlock so that efforts to bring about change to any one of them is often resisted in the others or in the system itself.

    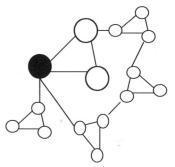

5. Usually one triangle in an interlocking system is primary, so that change in that one key triangle is more likely to induce change in the others.

6. One side of an emotional triangle tends to be more conflictual than the others. It is often the distribution and fluidity of conflict in a family that is crucial to its health rather than the quantity or the kind of issues that arise.

7. We can only change a relationship to which we belong. Therefore, the way to bring change to the relationship of two others is to try to maintain a well-defined relationship with each, and to avoid the responsibility for their relationship with one another.

Adapted from: Edwin H. Friedman, *Generation to Generation: Family Process in Church and Synagogue* (New York: The Guildford Press, 1985).

Family Genogram Timelines

Creating a timeline surrounding a nodal event or particular time period in the life of a family can help show development, patterns, progressions, and how certain events may have been a catalyst for people's responses. Use this worksheet to record significant events during a time period you want to explore. In chronological order record behaviors, transitions and moves (geographical, job, etc.), crises, historical events, illnesses, meetings, conversations, cutoffs, changes, nodal events (births, deaths, divorces), etc. Then, try to determine if there is a pattern, progression, or connection in the way you and/or your family members function during that period.

DATE: | EVENT:

Appendix C

The "20 Questions" To Ask About Your Family

You can use this list of twenty questions as an interview tool to help family members, or others, explore their genogram or to solicit information from family members about how they perceive these issues in your own family. (You may copy this page to share with family members for interview purposes).

1. In what ways did the birth order of the persons in your family affect relationships and functioning?

2. What was your role in the family system?

3. Who carried the legacy in the family system? Who is the standard bearer?

4. What assumptions about gender did your family of origin have?

5. Does your family system have an "illness of choice"? What is it?

6. What is the "family theme" or motto that comes closest to describing your family of origin?

7. How was anger expressed in your family of origin?

8. How was love expressed and communicated in your family?

9. What were you like in your family of origin when you were around 10 years old?

10. What was your perception of your parent's relationship when you were growing up?

11. Where do you see the major triangles in your family of origin?

12. Can you identify cutoffs in your family genogram?

13. In what ways do you see learned patterns of behavior (the ways you behave) in your family system playing out in your work system?

14. What is the ethnic background or heritage of your family of origin?

15. Can you identify an overfunction/underfunction reciprocity dynamic in your family of origin? In your current family?

16. How did your family handle crises?

17. What is the role and function of faith and religion in your family?

18. At what point in your family's lifecycle were you born? At what point did you "leave home"?

19. How did your family handle losses?

20. Does your family have a skeleton in the closet?

Source: Galindo, Boomer, Reagan, *A Family Genogram Workbook* (Educational Consultants, 2006).

Bibliography

Broderick, C. B. (1993). *Understanding Family Process: Basics Of Family Systems Theory.* Newbury Park, Calif., Sage Publications.

Daniels, D. N. and V. A. Price (2000). *The Essential Enneagram: The Definitive Personality Test And Self-Discovery Guide.* [San Francisco] HarperSanFrancisco.

Ebert, A. and M. Küstenmacher (1992). *Experiencing The Enneagram.* New York, Crossroad.

Galindo, Israel and Don Reagan (2005). *10 Best Parenting Ways To Ruin Your Teenager.* Richmond, VA: Educational Consultants.

Galindo, Israel (2001). *10 Best Parenting Ways To Ruin Your Child.* Richmond, VA: Educational Consultants.

Gilbert, Roberta (1992). *Extraordinary Relationships.* Minneapolis, MN: Wiley Press.

Gilbert, Roberta (2000). *Connecting With Our Children.* MN: Wiley Press.

Harper, J. M. and M. H. Hoopes (1990). *Uncovering Shame: An Approach Integrating Individuals And Their Family Systems.* New York, Norton.

Keyes, M. F. (1992). *Emotions And The Enneagram: Working Through Your Shadow Life Script.* Muir Beach, Calif., Molysdatur Publications.

Marlin, E. (1989). *Genograms: The New Tool For Exploring The Personality, Career, And Love Patterns You Inherit.* Chicago, Ill. Contemporary Books, 1989.

McGoldrick, M. (1995). *You Can Go Home Again: Reconnecting With Your Family.* New York: Norton.

Palmer, H. (1991). *The Enneagram: Understanding Yourself And The Others In Your Life.* [San Francisco] HarperSanFrancisco.

Richardson, Ronald W. (1984). *Family Ties Than Bind: A Self-Help Guide to Change Through Family of Origin Therapy.* Bellingham, Washington: International Self-Counsel Press Ltd.

Richardson, Ronald W. and Lois Richardson (1990). *Birth Order and You: How Your Sex and Position in the Family Affects Your Personality and Relationships.* Bellingham, Washington: International Self-Counsel Press Ltd.

Riso, D. R. (1990). *Understanding The Enneagram: The Practical Guide To Personality Types.* Boston, Houghton Mifflin.